MY NAME IS
MOSES

MY NAME IS
MOSES

ROBERT (BOB) HART

authorHOUSE®

AuthorHouse™
1663 Liberty Drive
Bloomington, IN 47403
www.authorhouse.com
Phone: 1-800-839-8640

Published by AuthorHouse   10/04/2012

ISBN: 978-1-4772-1650-7 (sc)
ISBN: 978-1-4772-3242-2 (e)

Library of Congress Control Number: 2012911643

INDEX

MY NAME IS MOSES

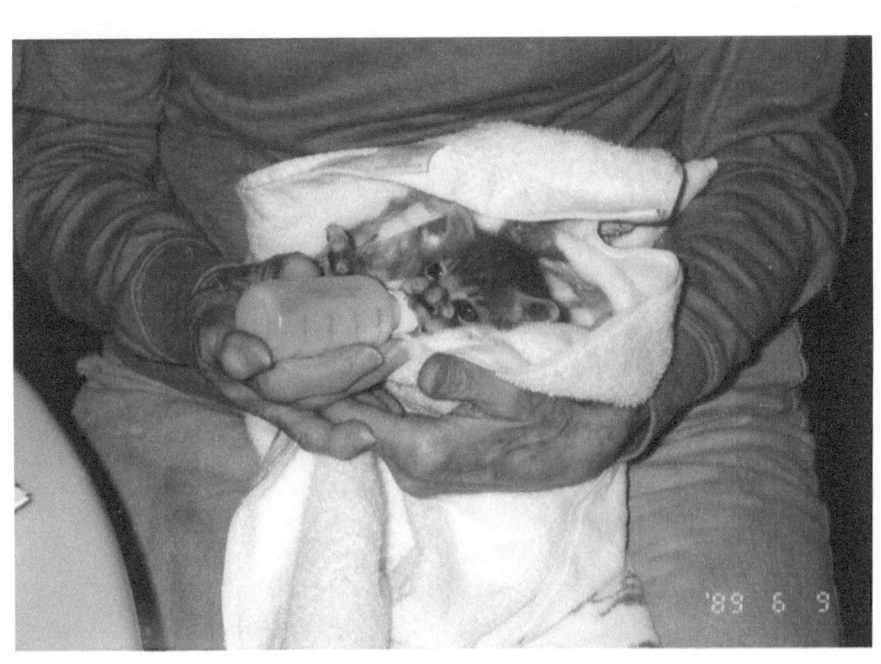

'89 6 9

I

I am all alone, in a small bed made of twigs and leaves. How I happen to be here, where I am, I really don't know. But one thing I do realize is that I am very cold and so terribly hungry. I am crying for help as loudly as I can, and have been doing so for so long that my voice is becoming hoarse. Won't someone—anyone—please hear me and help me?

Carrie has finally heard me crying. She is following the sounds to a place which is under a bush in a remote part of her rose garden. I am being picked up by her warm hands. That feels so good to me because my tiny body has become almost numbed by the cold. She is carrying me into her house now, and keeps on holding me in her warm hands to stop my shivering, and to warm my whole body. Now, will someone please give me something to eat! I'm starving, can't you see?

Carrie and Larry, together, are talking about how to feed me. They are trying to give me some cow's milk, using a small eyedropper. But I need to suck milk from a nipple in a natural way. Larry is calling a doctor (vetinarian) to find out how to feed me. He's going to her office now, to get whatever I need. He returns with some tiny baby bottles and little rubber nipples, and a good supply of the right kind of milk. Carrie is warming some of the milk, filling one of those tiny bottles, putting a nipple on it, and placing the soft rubber tip in my mouth. I'm supposed to start sucking. Good grief! I'm having a hard time holding onto that tiny nipple while at the same time trying to suck milk from it. I am tugging real hard on it! I am finally getting some milk, at last. I keep sucking.

After a little while my stomach stops hurting from being so hungry. After finishing my meal I feel groggy and fall asleep while in Carrie's warm hands.

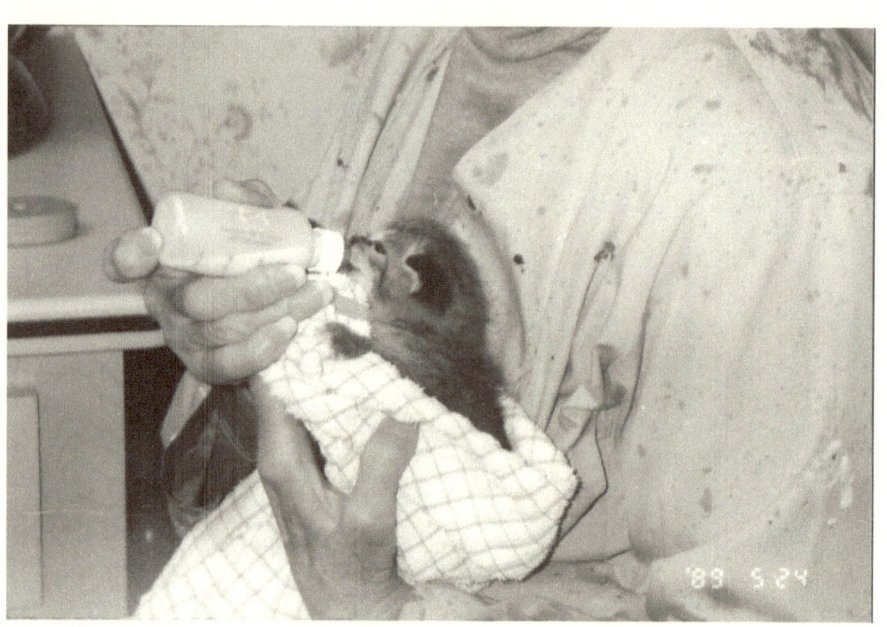

Larry says my cries for help while outside under a bush, sounded very much like a baby crocodile, but I'm not that. I guess my voice sounded strange because I had cried for such a long time, and so loudly.

My folks, Carrie and Larry, are fixing a small cardboard box, putting soft padding in the bottom, and placing my new bedroom on a heating pad. Carrie has warmed some beans in the oven, put them into one of Larry's socks, and has placed it into my bed beside me, so that I can cuddle up to it for warmth as needed. After being placed inside my new bedroom, where it's warm and cozy, I sleep there for a long time, until I wake up hungry, and ask for some more milk.

Carrie decides to name me "Moses", because I was found in a wilderness. I guess my namesake was also in that sort of place at one time long ago.

My folks say I am a kitten, but I don't feel like I am. I don't even know what that is. However, I surely don't look the same as they do. They are my family—I know no other! Carrie and Larry love me and treat me like I am their own. They take such good care of me. Carrie always helps me, keeps me clean, feeds me, sees that I stay warm and comfortable. I just seem to grow and become stronger all the time. Pretty soon I am seen crawling around on my cozy bedroom floor.

'89 5 24

II

When Carrie first found me, I was so very tiny. I couldn't see anything because my eyes were sealed shut. In a few days my eyes started to open, first just a little so I could see light, then slowly I could open my eyes wider. Carrie says my eyes are blue now, but the color may change as I become older. Carrie says I am cute, and her adorable darling kitten. She feeds me with that tiny nippled bottle. I often become very impatient when the milk doesn't come through the nipple fast enough. I sometimes pull on it so hard, trying to get the milk faster, but it doesn't seem to help very much. I always am sleepy after being fed, so Carrie gently puts me back in my padded box—my bedroom where it is always warm and cozy.

I know my legs are becoming stronger now, because I can stand on them without shaking. I was so weak earlier and became tired quickly. Now I can crawl easily, and even try to hang onto the towel Carrie has draped over the inside wall of my bedroom box.

I'm now able to crawl partway up the towel. I really want to see what is outside the walls of my bedroom. I'll just keep trying. I know I can get to the top sometime soon.

Wow! What do you know? I'm finally doing it! Now I find it's very hard to stay here, very near the top of this narrow wall, where it's easy to tip over, and fall to the floor below. I'm hanging on as tightly as I can, but here I am again, down at the bottom, and still in my bedroom. But I'll keep on trying—I know I'll get over the wall soon. I just need to eat more, grow some more and crawl around a lot more, so my four legs will get stronger than they are now.

Gee whiz! Now I am finally getting out of my box—my bedroom. Well, what do you know? The tile floor where I am is cold. Everything looks so different here. Carrie is nowhere to be seen. It is really scary. I am crawling a little way, but I don't know where to go. The cold floor is not at all like my cozy heated bedroom. I want to go back, but I don't know how. I am crying as loudly as I can. Finally Carrie hears me and comes quickly. She is gathering me up into her warm hands, cuddles me for a little while, and is now putting me back into my nice warm bedroom. I do not soon again try to leave my comfortable cozy bed.

I am so hungry again and am letting Carrie know that she should give me some more milk. That tiny rubber nipple is now too small. Besides, I can't get milk from it fast enough to satisfy my growing appetite. I am now getting some sharp teeth. Biting the nipple to hang onto it, has finally made it give me milk more freely. Carrie says I must have bitten a hole in it, now that the milk comes faster for me.

Now that I'm able to bite things, Carrie has started giving me some solid food—not just milk alone. I now no-longer want to suck on that nipple. I am learning to lap milk from a saucer. Now I can eat and drink whenever I want to.

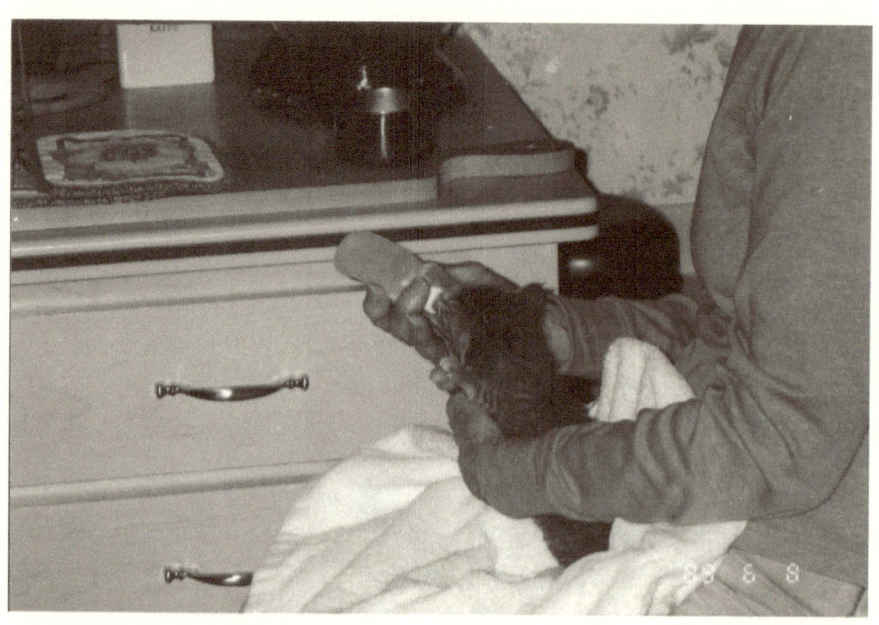

III

Time passes so quickly. I'm a little bigger now, and I'm stronger, steadier on my legs, and can walk and not just crawl as I did a while back. I now can leave my bedroom whenever I want to.

I am learning to run. Carrie is throwing a small red soft rubber ball for me to chase. I have lots of fun doing that. I soon find it's easy to pick the ball up in my mouth, and carry it back to Carrie, so that she can toss it away again for me to chase, pick up and bring back to her. We have a lot of fun together doing that. Carrie says I really look cute, when I carry that red ball in my mouth while on my way back to her.

Carrie says that I'm a little boy kitten. I have a soft grey coat of hair, and some, but not all, white fur on my feet. Where the fur is white my toes are plnk, and where the fur is grey my toes are black. The reason I can climb so easily is because my toenails are sharp and curved downward. They can easily hook into things—towels and other soft stuff.

I have ten or so, long straight whiskers that extend from each of my cheeks. Also, I have three or four straight hairs, my eyebrows, above each eye. My chest and stomach fur is white and very fine and soft. I have a tail that I can move in any way I want. Its fur is light grey with very dark grey rings that run around its length. I use my tail to tell my folks how I feel about all sorts of things. For instance, I wave it gently from side to side while held upright, to give a friendly greeting to Carrie or Larry. I sometimes twitch or shake my tail very fast when I'm not quite sure about going outside when it is cold out there. When either Carrie or Larry talk to me, in their special voice tones meant especially for me while I'm lying on a rug or robe next to them, I answer them by wiggling the very tip of my tail. If they keep talking to me, then I move my whole tail really fast from side to side, and sometimes up and down. While doing this, I don't even have to raise my head—they know I'm answering them by using tail movements only.

IV

While in the house, my folks do crazy things that are hard for me to explain. For instance, they take a big round object from a closet. It has six short legs to hold it above the floor, and they take turns getting onto it and jumping up and down. They call that thing a "Rebounder". It is really springy when they jump on it. I have tried to do it with them too, but I don't like it very much. I would rather just lie down on it when no-one is jumping up and down on it. It is a nice cool and comfortable place to rest and snooze.

Larry does such strange things early each morning. He lies down on the carpet and moves his arms and legs about, reaching as far as he can. He does this for quite a while. Also, he does this while standing up—why? I don't know.

He tries to touch his toes, but can't reach down that far. Sometimes I try to catch his foot as it swings near to where I happen to be. Once in a while I lie down next to his feet, while he's doing standing movements. He calls this his morning "Exercises".

I sometimes get bored, so I go to a window that's covered by a shade, and by standing on my back legs, use my front legs and feet to make the shade rattle against the window. Larry always has to stop what he's doing while exercising, to make me stop my efforts to get his attention. I do get his attention, for sure, but it doesn't help very much, because I get scolded. I know I should not do it, but getting his attention for a while is well worth the scolding I receive.

V

My back legs are very strong now. I can quickly and easily jump up onto a chair or table. It's so much fun to jump and play. Carrie sometimes lets me go outside into the yard when the sun is shining. The rose garden is fenced to prevent strangers—animals of all kinds—from damaging plants as they dig for worms and grubs. The fence is as high as Carrie is tall, so I am not supposed to go out of that area.

I am curious to see what is beyond that fence. I do have strong legs, made especially for the purpose of jumping, so I spring to the top, and drop to the ground on the other side. I wander all around, smelling plants, investigating everything. I've found a nice place under a tree where it's shadey, so I lie down for a nap.

When Carrie discovers that I've left her garden, she is very upset. She is calling me, over and over again, but I just keep quiet—it is so pleasant, just resting and sleeping right where I am. Looking for me are both Carrie and Larry. They finally find where I am. I'm scolded, being picked up and carried back into the house.

I'm not allowed to go outside for quite a while. They know I am sad, and want to go out again. Finally, Carrie lets me go, but stays in the garden with me all the while. She's trying to watch me. When she's busy with her flowers, I manage to slip away, and over the fence I go. I just wander about the outer yard. I soon learn to jump back into the rose garden. It is so interesting to roam about while outside. I wander farther from the house, but always know my way back home.

'89 7

VI

Remembering the fun I have, chasing the little red ball while playing with Carrie, when outside there are birds and small animals moving about, so I also chase and try to catch them. Once in a while, one is caught. They always wiggle and squirm, trying to get away from me. I just want to play with them, and usually do for a while. Carrie has found out what I'm doing, severely scolds me, and says I must not do that, and that I have to stop. But how can I stop? It is so much fun chasing and trying to catch things that run or fly about as these animals and birds do! It seems like I am just meant to keep right on doing it! I can't resist it! I am often scolded.

I see a bird high up in an oak tree. It just keeps coming and going to a nest she has built far out on a limb. I am curious to know why that bird is doing that. I have to find out. It is easy to climb the tree, so up I go. Just as I am nearing that bird's nest, Carrie discovers what I'm up to, because the bird sees me and screams at me, and is flying at me, trying to peck me. Carrie calls to me, loudly saying, "Leave that bird alone!" But I am not obeying her at all. I keep edging closer to that nest. Carrie reaches for a garden hose, turns the faucet on full force, and soaks me to the skin until I am willing to back away from that bIrd and her nest. Carrie keeps soaking me until I am clear out of the tree, and am running away as fast as I can. I am so wet, it takes a very long time to dry my thick fur.

VII

Often now, while outside the rose garden, I wander farther and farther away from home. There are other fences that I jump over. It is so very interesting to see what is on the other side, and beyond. Often I find a good place to lie down and sleep. Time passes so quickly. I may stay away too long, causing Carrie and Larry to worry about me. Once in a while I stay away so long that the sun is setting, and it is starting to get dark. By that time, I'm hungry for a good meal. My folks are concerned for my safety, and they tell me so.

While I am wandering about, a long way from home, a big ugly orange colored animal, shaped like I am, but twice my size, wants to fight with me. Never having fought, I don't know how. Besides, this critter is much too large! I'm running home as fast as I can, back over the fence into the rose garden, but he has caught up with me, and has bitten me really hard on my tail right near my back legs. He jumps the fence with me, and together we cross through the garden to the opposite side, jumping over that fence also. There's a large oak tree, just beyond the fence, so I run up into that tree, and climb as high as possible, onto a small limb that's able to support my weight, but not his. He is still trying to get to me!

Carrie is in the rose garden while all of this is happening, and she hears my cries for help. She opens the gate, sees where I am, and that orange beast also. That mean snarling beast is a target, a threat that must be eliminated! Carrie gets a garden hose with a spray nozzle, turning on the faucet full force, and soaking that critter while it is near the tree's top. Carries target, by now soaked to the skin, loses its hold on the limb, and comes tumbling down, all the way to the hard ground.

Running away as fast as it can, we've not seen it ever again.

I am so high up in the tree, I am afraid to come back down. I learn then and there, it's easier to climb up than it is to climb down. Claws are of little help while descending an oak tree. Carrie and Larry are spending a lot of time, trying to convince me that the danger is past, and that I should try to come back down out of that tree. Carrie talks me down to a place where, while standing on a ladder, she can reach up, and take me by my front legs and chest. She lifts me out of the tree and places me back onto the ground. What a terrible experience this has been!

My tail is really sore where I was bitten. I'm doing all I can by licking the wound. My folks don't know, because they haven't seen my tail where I've worn most of the fur off by my licking it so often. I am really sick now, and Carrie is noticing, lifts my tail, exposes the infected area, and decides right now to take me to the vetinarian. I hate riding in the truck. Everything moves past me so fast, I'm being given a shot to kill the infection. Now we can go back home, and wait for my tail to heal. I'm feeling better now that a week has passed, but I'm told it'll take a year or more to grow my fur back to cover the bare skin.

VIII

Sometimes Carrie and Larry let me go outside with them, into the outer yard. They walk all of the way around the house. They just keep doing that, time after time. It seems kind of silly to me. They want me to do that too. I know that is so because they keep calling my name, "Moses", and keep coaxing me along. So I try to do as they want. I seem to get tired before they do, and then I fall behind. Then I begin to take shortcuts across places where the distance is not as great. That makes good sense, don't you think? Finally I just sit down and wait for them to come past me on their next time around. If I'm not too tired, I might even run really fast, to catch up with.them. After a while, they seem to tire, and then we all go back into the house so we can rest on soft carpeting or chair cushions.

IX

I have just now jumped out of the rose garden, because I can hear a large number of birds talking to each other; They are on the other side of a different very high fence, and in a neighbor's yard where they are being fed each morning. I have found a place where I can crawl under the fence, so I can go into the yard next door. A whole flock of birds is there. Each bird is busy picking food off the ground, and making a lot of noise while doing it. Carrie has said they are "Quail". I am trying to sneak up on one of them. Without my knowing it, the neighbor is watching. I might have been seen in that yard before—that's quite possible. Suddenly I hear a loud noise and at the same moment I feel a sharp pain. I go home as fast as I can, but the pain follows and stays with me for a very long time. I didn't tell my folks about it, because I don't know how.

Larry often strokes the fur on my back, as he is doing right now. He feels a lump right where my fur should be smooth. He has to know why. He spreads my fur apart over the lump, exposing my skin. He has found that I was shot by a pellet gun. The lead pellet is buried in my skin, but a tiny bit of it can still be seen. Larry gets something sharp to use for digging that slug out. It hurts quite a lot while he's doing it, but I guess it's better out than for it to still be stuck in my skin.

Larry told Carrie that in fact he had heard the noise made by that pellet gun when it was fired, and that the sound had come from that neighbor's yard. Larry says it is not legal to do such shooting, and should not have been done. My wound is healing without becoming infected. I am getting over it pretty fast, and have decided not to go back there again. Carrie says I should not have been there in the first place.

X

I've just left the rose garden again. I'm going to travel someplace different today. I'm always having to jump over fences, no matter where I go. Carrie is always concerned for my safety. She says there are predators around that can cause serious problems, so be watchful always. She mentioned "Coyotes". I don't know much about them, having never seen any. They howl really loudly. They travel in packs. Sometimes one may get separated, from the rest of the pack, and it howls so that the others howl in response. Then the lost coyote finds its way back to join its buddies.

Here is another fence I must jump over. I've not seen this one before. It's a little higher than most. Over I go!

Ouch! I'm caught on something! It's sticking into my belly! It won't let go!

I'm trying to wiggle free, but something sharp is jabbing into my belly, just forward from my back legs. I can feel it ripping my skin—now it's becoming more painful. I've got to tear myself loose, and go back home. I can't get myself off without hurting myself even more. But I must, or I'll be here forever!

I cry for help, but none comes. Finally, I manage to rip myself loose from the thing, and endure excruciating pain while doing it. I'm bleeding badly as I walk home. What will Carrie say?

Although suffering beyond belief, I jump back into the rose garden, where I sit down to examine my wound. It looks to be really bad! It has stopped bleeding. I lick it, hoping to make it feel better and make it heal. I won't let either of my folks know what has happened. I'll just keep on licking it to help heal it.

I'm beginning to feel sick now. It's been quite a while since this happened to me. I'm still licking it, but it's getting no better. I'm in the house doing that, when Carrie sees what I am doing. She makes me show her what I've been licking, and why. By now, there's no sign of healing. Instead, the wound is badly inflamed and infected.

Larry is shown my problem and immediately calls for an emergency appointment with the vetinarian. We head for her office. She examines me thoroughly, cleans up and dresses my deep wound, and I'm given antibiotics to kill the infection. Now I am waiting to feel well again.

We are all back home again. I'm still licking my gradually healing sore belly. It is beginning to look and feel better, but has made a very swollen place on my belly. After all infection is gone, there's a part of me that's still not the same as it was before my injury.

I've now learned that it is necessary to be very careful when doing such things as going over fences. After my recent injury, my folks have decided I must not go outside any more. I am really upset about that, and tell them so! Still, they won't let me go into the rose garden, because I always go over the fence, into the outer yard, and beyond.

Larry and Carrie are busy raising the fence, right where I had been crossing, so that I can finally be kept at home, safe from danger and further injury. I have to accept what they say, and soon become happy again. My folks really do try to do whatever is best for me. I know they love me a lot! I always try to show my love for them, and let them know I do.

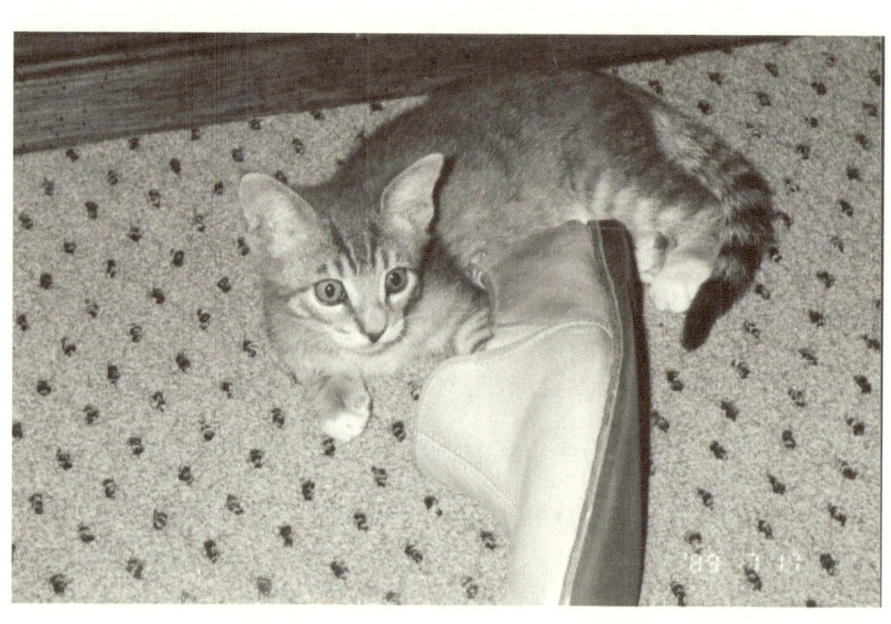

XI

I often coax when I want to go outside. Sometimes they let me, and othertimes they say no. In fact, "No" is the first word I learned. My folks talk to each other by making a wide variety of sounds, most of which I don't understand. However, some words they say to me often, I know what they mean. "Num—num" means I'm being offered something good to eat, which I like and want. When they ask if I want to go out into the rose garden, they usually just say "Outside"? I often answer by saying "Yes", in my own soft voice. When I have a hard time getting someone's attention who is nearby, I simply walk to the door, reach up to the door knob and rattle it a bit to make a little noise. Usually someone notices and then opens the door for me. When I want to come back into the house, I just come to the door and sit down and wait. I send thoughts to them which they seem to receive, because I do not usually have to wait very long.

There is one large oak tree in the rose garden. It's right next to an arbor that Larry built to shade a part of the garden. I like to climb that tree to get up onto the top of the arbor. While up there, I can see far away things that are in other yards, and places I used to visit before being stopped from leaving the rose garden. Now I don't get hurt anymore like I used to. I know my folks always want me to stay safe.

I like to lie down in the sunshine while on the arbor. Also, the oak tree provides shade, so I can stay as warm or as cool as I like, just by moving a little way on top of the arbor.

It's really easier for me to climb up the oak tree than it is for me to come back down, because my claws are shaped only for climbing. I can't come down head first, so I have to turn almost sideways to get a grip on the tree trunk. Carrie often stands beneath the tree to take me off the tree trunk after I've gotten down far enough for her to reach me. She takes me by my front legs and chest, and gently puts me down onto the ground. Sometimes I have to get all the way down by myself, which is really hard for me. I find that I have to jump quite a way down onto the ground, when I can no longer hold onto the tree trunk.

I really do like to go into the rose garden while it's dark outside, before the sun begins to rise in the morning. I can see very well, even in the dark. Many small creatures move about in the yard at night, making different sounds which I find very exciting. I might even catch something to play with, without Carrie knowing about it!

Many different kinds of animals visit our outer yard, where there's no fencing. There are lots of deer and javelinas, and once in a while I may happen to see a rabbit, skunk, chipmonk, squirrel or fox. Birds I've seen are of many kinds, but most are quail. They stay on the ground most of the time. They can run very fast, and when they fly, their wings make lots of noise while passing through the air. That's why I like to chase them. They talk to each other; making all kinds of different sounds while searching for food. I love to scare them into the air—that's very exciting! Carrie does not want me to chase any of the birds at all.

'89 8 5

XII

I never need to wear anything over my warm fur coat. It keeps me cozy, even when it's very cold outside. The only times when I don't enjoy being outside is when water falls from the sky. My folks call that "Rain". Once in a while something white drifts down slowly from the sky. It is soft and cold, and gets wet when I put my feet in it. Carrie calls it "Snow". It always turns into water when the sun shines on it.

I love to sit on a window sill where I can see birds and other things moving about in the outer yard. I can't play with them, but it's fun just to watch. It's next best to being out there with them. Carrie does not want me to hurt other living creatures. I really don't mean to, but sometimes I just play too roughly. That's because I'm so much bigger than they are. I really don't mean to hurt them—just have some fun.

'89 6 5

XIII

Some wild animals are just outside the large front window where I am sitting and watching. They are very near the front door. My folks call them "Pigs", but say they are really "Javelinas". They travel and forage for food in large family herds. Some are very big and fat, while others are of a whole range of sizes down to quite small. They are damaging plants very near to where I am sitting. Larry sees them too.

Now Larry is walking toward the front door. I think he's going to open the door to chase them away. Instead, there's a very loud noise. Larry has struck the door suddenly, so hard that it practically scares me out of my skin. It has caused every hair on my body to stand on end and straight away from my body. My hair is standing up like that for a long time. Carrie and Larry are about laughing themselves silly. They say only on "Halloween" have they ever seen such a sight, and then only in pictures. My fur coat usually stays close to my body, but when it's cold, and I'm outside, I can fluff it up a bit to keep me somewhat warmer. But when something happens that I least expect, BOY! That makes my hairs all stand straight up, without my even knowing it or thinking about it. Larry says when that happens it's called an "Involuntary spontaneous reaction" which is meant to scare away any wild animal that might be threatening my safety or life.

XIV

My folks sometimes go away for long periods of time. I can tell when that's going to happen. They put on different coverings, called "Clothing", and change things on their feet, called "Shoes". Carrie takes a large colored bag along with her, and bundles up to stay warm. When they come back, they have lots of bags which are carried into the house. I usually check into those that are set on the floor. I know some of the stuff is food for me, because they always have some on hand to feed me when it's time.

Carrie and Larry bring all kinds of good nourishment for me. There are meat flavors, such as tuna, salmon, beef and chicken. Also, I have dried foods that offer a variety of tastes. My very most favorite is like dessert. I could eat a lot of that, but Carrie won't let me, because she says it will make me too fat. Carrie always keeps a bowl full of fresh water for me to have as I need it. I lap quite a lot of it, which helps when I eat dry food. Carrie always has a separate bowl of water for her own use when she works on different kinds of things, called "Crafts". I really like best, drinking from Carrie's bowl—I guess that's because it's hers, and I really like being right where she happens·to be.

'89 8 /1

XV

I sometimes feel very frisky, and to get Carrie's attention I suddenly run and jump against Carrie's legs, then quickly leap away, out of her reach. She runs after me but can't catch me because I run faster than she does. I always surprise her because I do it when she's busy doing things, such as preparing a meal. She knows I'm only playing with her, so she joins the fun. She chases me, then stops and goes back to doing as before. When I'm sure she's not watching me, I run and jump against her legs another time, and again she runs after me. We have lots of fun together. She seems to know I like being chased from one room to another.

Lots of times I play with her shoes while she's sitting, watching and listening to television. I'm, always careful not to hurt her with my sharp teeth and toenails. She calls my toenails "Claws" because they hook into soft things and hang on until I want to let go.

I like to tease Carrie because it causes her to chase me. I sometimes walk kind of sideways, with my back raised a bit higher in its middle, and with my tail arched off to one side. It always makes Carrie laugh because it looks so funny, she says.

One of the things I really enjoy is snuggling up on Carrie 's lap. She usually covers with a very soft laprobe. I first ask for her permission, and to do I that I walk onto her lap from an adjacent table, look up into her eyes to see if it's okay with her, and then push down into her lap with first one front foot, then the other, over and over again for several minutes, while at the same time purring contentedly. After I've done that, I settle down into a very comfortable position and continue purring softly. Carrie likes to hear me purr, because then she knows I like her so very much, and that I'm as happy as I can be—very satisfied being right where I am. Carrie says my purr sounds like a tiny engine might sound.

XVI

From time to time, Carrie cleans the floors and carpets throughout the house. She uses a thing that connects into the wall with a long cord. When she triggers a switch on the handle, it roars so loudly that it scares me, so I run and hide. The best and safest place I can find is behind bookcases in Carrie's hobby room. It's dark there, and the quietest place I've found so far.

When Carrie has cleaned the rest of the house, and finally has only her workroom left to clean, she guesses correctly where I am hiding. She picks me up and carries me to another part of the house that she's already cleaned. Carrie is so very thoughtful and caring, and does everything she can to please me. She knows how very much I detest, even hate, that thing she calls a "Vacuum sweeper".

XVII

Carrie and Larry often go out into the rose garden, to sit together on a wide hanging bench, called a "Swing". The graveled path in front of it, is usually warmed by the sun. I love to lie there, in front of them, and roll back and forth. It feels so good! I just keep turning from one side to the other. Usually some rose leaves, or other stuff, sicks onto my thick fur. When we all get ready to go back into the house, I have to let either Carrie or Larry brush me off, or sometimes use a damp paper towel on my fur, to keep me from getting the house dirty by stuff that might fall off my coat.

At a certain time of year, I start to shed my winter coat of hair. That's so I won't be too warm during the summer heat. Then, when the weather starts cooling, as winter approaches, I start growing new fur for colder days. Carrie uses a stiff bristle brush that pulls loose hair out of my coat. It feels good when she first starts brushing, so I purr. After a little while it feels like the brush is pulling on hair that's still attached to my skin. Then I try to move away, telling Carrie I want her to quit brushing me. A lot of loose hair has to be combed from the brush before I can again be brushed at a later time.

XVIII

Every once in a while, Carrie reaches up into a high cupboard and brings down three shiney things—one has a handle that turns around and around, another is round and has gougers all over it, and the other has three legs and black feet. She puts them all together, and calls it a "Grating machine".

When that's done, she takes an orange package from the refrigerator and opens it to uncover what's inside. She then cuts a thick slice off, covers the cut end of what's left with wax paper and returns it to cold storage. It's the piece she cut off that is exciting for me. Carrie calls this stuff "Cheese".

Larry puts that large piece of cheese into the top of the grater and begins to turn the handle, which shreds the cheese and lets it fall into a large shiney bowl. Once in a while a piece breaks off from the larger piece, and that part is for me.

If I happen to be somewhere else when they're grating cheese, either Larry or Carrie will call out, "Cheesey" loudly, and I know that means they are going to give me a treat that I really do like, so I come running as fast as I can. They usually give me several small pieces which I eat with great pleasure. So you see, the word "Cheesey" is still one more word that I have learned and know well.

XIX

Larry always comes out from the bedroom quite early each morning. I like to greet him by walking up beside him and lying on the floor, waiting for him to pet me. I really love for him to scratch my forehead and beneath my chin, where I can't do it myself.

Sometimes Larry sits at the library table to write, and other times sits at his desk attending to business matters. On these occasions, I love to lie on the desk or table, right in front of him, just to be near because I like him so much. He's always so good to me, and gives me attention which I want.

Larry and Carrie both understand what I say, mostly by what they call "Body language"—movements I make with my tail, or where I go and wait to be noticed. They always seem to know what I mean, without my having to speak out-loud.

Often when I've been in the rose garden for quite a long while, Larry knocks on the window a few times to let me know I can come back into the house if I want to. I know I don't have to go unless it's my own desire to do so. If I don't want to go, I just stay where I am.

Often, when I do go back into the house, if I ask, Larry will give me some delicious treats. I know where they're kept, so all I have to do is jump up onto a low shelf. or simply wait below that shelf, and either Larry or Carrie will get some of the treat morsels out for me to enjoy—they are so tasteyl

XX

Now, I've told you all about life, myself and family, and daily affairs. I am so very lucky to be where I am. I can stay warm when it's freezing cold outside, and I can lie in the sunshine or shade when weather is warm.

My folks look after my every need—food, water, a good home—and they keep me safe from the perils of the outside world. I sometimes feel that they are my personal servants. But there's a great deal more to it than that. I try to make them happy too. I make them laugh, and try to do as they want me to do. I try to keep myself clean by licking my fur coat. I try to stay close to each of them, so that they know I really do care about them a lot. I really love them just as much as they love me.

Each of us is so very fortunate to have the others. It just could not be any better than it is for all of us!

AFTERWORD

We, Carrie and Larry, would like the readers of ` "MY NAME IS MOSES", to know that all that Moses has related to you, is based on absolute fact.

It is our priviledge to know Moses as a person with whom we share our lives. He is as close to being human as he can be, without his actually being so. He can uncannily tell us exactly what he wants, and what he expects from us, from hour to hour and day to day. He's now been with us more than nine years, and continues to be our wonderful companion. Sometimes at meal time he expects personal service, rising onto his four legs, and waiting to be picked up and carried by lying across Larry's two arms, then placed by his food bowl. Larry calls this "Taxi service".

Long ago, when Moses was one year old, Carrie felt that Moses needed a companion like himself, so one was acquired. Moses was visibly disturbed by our bringing in another so unlike himself—he would have nothing at all to do with Carrie, who was responsible, for at least two weeks. Even to this day, he has not fully accepted Sam as his living companion.

Sam's natural instinct is to be overly sociable, and Moses emphatically rejects such behavior, and obviously regards him as being too invasive into personal space. They are not pals at all.

We speculate that in his afterlife, Moses may in fact return in human form. He certainly has strong leanings in that direction.

Moses is the most intelligent of his kind that we've ever known. He is our pride and joy every day of our lives. We are so very thankful that he came to us the way he did.

When you think about it, no wonder Moses is so like a human—after all, the only family he has ever known since birth are us two, Carrie and Larry, in effect his true parents.